Exotic Plants
Pure Love
To:
from:

Every challenge, every adversity, contains within it the seeds of opportunity and growth

Roy T. Bennett

Don't judge each day by the harvest you reap but by the seeds that you plant

Robert Louis Stevenson

I hope that while so many people are out smelling the flowers, someone is taking the time to plant some

Herbert Rappaport

Plant and reap what
comes from your heart
and you will never know
what sadness is

Alan Maiccon

You can get attached to
plants when you lose
faith in people

Manuele Fior

In order to bloom you
have to be planted first

Giovannie de Sadeleer

Look at a tree, a plant.
How still they are, how
deeply rooted in being.
Allow nature to teach
you stillness

Eckhart Tolle

Plants are filterless solar

powered air purifiers

Khang Kijarro Nguyen

I only plant seeds,
it's up to you to nurture
them and let them grow

Harken Headers

Sow the seeds of hard work and you will reap the fruits of success.

Find something to do, do it with all your concentration. You will excel

Israelmore Ayivor

Plant seeds of kindness
and watch your
blessings flow
abundantly

Charmaine J Forde

Never plant a seed that seems good to eyes despite plant a seed that will be a shed in the sunlight

Merlin Thomas

Anyone who will eat his seeds today will be hungry tomorrow because he has nothing to plant and nothing to harvest later

Israelmore Ayivor

Whatever a man sow,
shall he reap

Lailah Gifty Akita

Use the dirt life throws
at you to plant the seeds
of your success

Matshona Dhliwayo

Plant love,

let it sprout

H.S. Crow

I water my plants until they drown & this is the only way I know how to love

Nitya Prakash

You were born with the seeds of success and happiness, but nobody else but yourself could plant them in your life

Edmond Mbiaka

Bloom where you are
planted and sow where
you are fed

Stella Payton